Kids Yoga

More Animals ™

Our Newest Yogi

_____

Digital DesignZ
PUBLISHING & GRAPHICS Inc.

Published by Digital Designz, Inc.
KidsYoga is a registered trademark of Digital Designz, Inc.
For more information, our website is: www.Kids-Yoga.net or email: info@Kids-Yoga.net.
ISBN 978-1-7367600-8-6
ISBN 978-1-7367600-9-3 (electronic)

KidsYoga is a series of books depicting
yoga poses for young children. This book
is based on animals, each animal has a
pose and sound a child could make.
It's a fun way to learn yoga
for young children ages two to six.

Table of Contents

Flamingo

From a standing position, put weight on right leg. Grab your left foot with left hand, then bring your right hand up. Now try your other leg.

Can you "Honk" like a Flamingo?

Gorilla

Bend at your waist. Tuck your hands under your toes.
Bend your knees if needed.

Can you "Grunt" like a Gorilla?

Stork

Stand with your arms stretched out. With weight on left leg, lift and bend right knee. Then switch to the other side.

10

Can you "Chirp" like a Stork?

Lizard

Begin in a down dog shape (hands and feet on the floor). Bring right knee forward and come to a lunge position. Go down on your elbows. Switch sides, bring left knee forward.

Can you "Hissss" like a Lizard?

Camel

Kneel on the floor, knees apart and feet are flat.
Lean back and try to grab your ankles.

Can you "Burrrr" like a Camel?

Tiger

On all fours, tuck in right knee to chest. Then moving your bent knee towards the sky, look up. Now switch to your left side.

16

Can you "Purr" like a Tiger?

Lion

Kneel down sitting back on your heals. Bring your hands
to your thighs and spread your fingers, ready to roar.

Can you "Roooar" like a Lion?

Turtle

Sit on the ground, legs separated wide with knees bent.
Place palms on the floor and slide your arms under your knees.
Bend your head towards the ground (pretend you're in your shell).

Can you "Hide" like a Turtle?

Eagle

Sit and cross your legs on the floor. Wrap your arms tightly and touch your hands together. Then switch your position.

Can you "Eeeer" like an Eagle?

Pigeon

Down on all fours, slide right knee forward and to the right. Straighten left leg back and point your toe. Then lower your hips and straighten your arms, now look up. Go ahead and switch sides.

Can you "CooCoo" like a Pigeon?

About the Author

Linda Sakevich, affectionately
known as Ms. Linda,
is a physical education teacher
at a private school.
She's introducing yoga
to children by
combining her love
of teaching with yoga.

Namasté

Kids Yoga™

More Animals

Kids Yoga™

Subscribe to our book club
and be the first to
get our new series and
receive our Spinner Game!

For more information or to be notified
when this next book is to released
go to www.Kids-Yoga.Net
or email us at info@Kids-Yoga.Net

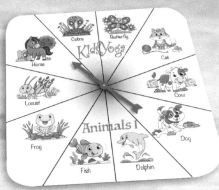

Try our new Spinner Game

CPSIA information can be obtained
at www.ICGtesting.com
Printed in the USA
BVHW012106170223
658740BV00008B/625